GW00370409

THE GREAT
GLOUCESTERSHIRE
FLOOD
2007

THE GREAT GLOUCESTERSHIRE FLOOD

2007

A GLOUCESTERSHIRE
MEDIA PUBLICATION

Frontispiece: Sandhurst residents are rescued as the floodwaters rise. 760290-4

First published 2007
© Gloucestershire Media, 2007

The right of Gloucestershire Media to be identified as the Author of this work has been asserted in accordance with the Copyrights, Designs and Patents Act 1988.

All rights reserved. No part of this book may be reprinted or reproduced or utilised in any form or by any electronic, mechanical or other means, now known or hereafter invented, including photocopying and recording, or in any information storage or retrieval system, without the permission in writing from the Publishers.

British Library Cataloguing in Publication Data.
A catalogue record for this book is available from the British Library.

ISBN 978 0 7524 4586 1

Typesetting and origination by NPI Media Group for Gloucestershire Media.
Printed in Great Britain

Contents

Acknowledgements

The photographs in this book were taken by Gloucestershire Media staff photographers Mikal Ludlow, Robert Davis, Paul Nicholls, Simon Pizzey, Anna Lythgoe, Daniel Martino, Daniel Istitene, James Douglas, Martin Perry and Michael Smith.

Freelancers: Antony Thompson (www.atp-photo.com), Shaun Thompson (www. st-images.co.uk), South West News Service (www.swns.com), Bruce Seabrooke (www. gpaimages.com), Press Association.

County residents: Rebekah Stephens, Rob Keene, Abi Pates, Clinton Mogridge, Neil Phelps, Mark Playne, Stuart Strathearn and Craig Guthrie.

Thanks also to the Chief Constable, Dr Tim Brain, Chief Fire Officer Terry Standing and Editor of *The Citizen*, Ian Mean, for their contribution to this book.

With thanks to all those county residents, members of the emergency services, the military, volunteer rescue agencies and everyone who was affected by the floods who coped so stoically in the face of adversity.

Compiled by Matt Holmes

Introduction

The Great Gloucestershire Flood had its beginnings in the deluge of rain that started falling on Friday, July 20 and over the next 24 hours, nearly six inches had fallen on what was already a very rain-sodden county.

What happened then is hopefully encapsulated - mainly through dramatic and very human pictures - in this book Gloucestershire Media decided to publish to mark a truly astonishing month in the life of the county.

It was a month when we witnessed great courage of the emergency services in rescuing people from the floods and real bravery in holding back those relentless floodwaters in extreme conditions to ensure that the county retained its power, and eventually restored the supply of fresh water from the tap.

It was the legendary editor of the *Daily Express*, Arthur Christiansen, who coined the phrase: "One picture is worth a thousand words". That is why we have decided to tell the story of the Great Gloucestershire Flood 2007 mainly by pictures - through the lenses of our superb photographic team at *The Citizen*, *The Gloucestershire Echo*, *The Forester*, our news agency colleagues and the many people who sent in their dramatic pictures to our website, www.thisisgloucestershire.co.uk, as this amazing story of the floods unfolded.

Was it really conceivable in 2007 that this prosperous county could be virtually brought to its knees by the floodwaters?

Truly it was. In those dark, damp early days following the weekend deluge over Friday, Saturday and Sunday, July 20-22, we were within two inches of becoming the focus of the largest evacuation of people in peacetime Britain.

If the Fire and Rescue services and forces' personnel had not won the battle to save the Walham electricity switching station near Gloucester being engulfed by the floodwaters, the Army was on the brink of evacuating large areas of the county to the West Midlands. With thousands of people without fresh water, the loss of Walham would have meant no electricity for the whole of the county plus parts of South Wales. It was almost a doomsday scenario, and as Chief Fire and Rescue officer Terry Standing writes in his piece about the battle to save Walham, the loss of that power would have almost certainly led to deaths.

As it was, thankfully, fatalities were minimal with 19-year-old Mitchell Taylor swept away in Tewkesbury on that first Friday of the floods and father and son Bram and Chris Lane tragically losing their lives at a rugby club in Tewkesbury, as they attempted to pump water from the flood-hit clubhouse. When you look through the pictures in this book, it is remarkable that more lives were not lost directly as a result of that floodwater which devastated more than 5,000 properties in the area.

I remember flying over Gloucester and Tewkesbury during the first week of the flooding in an Army helicopter, and the picture on the front page of this book paints the picture so well. It was horrifying to see just how many homes, particularly in the Tewkesbury area, had obviously been built on the flood plain. They were almost marooned, like the town's historic Abbey. It was a vivid illustration if any were needed that one of the major questions to be asked by Sir Michael Pitt's government inquiry into the flooding - both here in Gloucestershire and in Yorkshire - must surround the future of building new homes on the flood plain.

What new planning regulations can be introduced to prevent this flood plain building and, at the same time, provide the new homes the county so desperately needs?

Do we need to make changes to our infrastructure to cope with future flooding? How can our rivers, water courses, drains and ditches be maintained more effectively to stave off flooding?

There are many questions like these that must be answered, and one of the most urgent surrounds the Severn Trent Water authority. Why didn't they have an emergency contingency plan to protect fresh water in Gloucestershire? Severn Trent has a great deal to answer. Many of us were without any fresh water from the tap for nearly three weeks as a direct result of the flooding of its Mythe water treatment works situated precariously on the banks of the Severn at Tewkesbury.

And as this book goes to press, Severn Trent is literally still in the eye of the storm over its refusal to pay compensation for the lack of fresh water. The indications from many of our readers are that they are unwilling to accept lightly that they will receive nothing in the way of compensation for their inconvenience.

The bill to Gloucestershire County Council for this catastrophe is at least £55m with £25m of that figure alone needed to be spent on the county's flood damaged roads. Money is coming in from the Government in dribs and drabs, but there is, so far, little sign of the large amounts of cash we need to restore the infrastructure. We will continue to battle with Government to ensure money flows into the county.

However, the great flood has thrown up something of a benefit which no Government money could ever buy. That is a renewal of community spirit in many areas. The water bowsers on street corners had the effect in many places of encouraging neighbours to perhaps mix with each other properly for the first time. Yes, there was probably a sense of wartime spirit and certainly a rekindling of neighbourliness which helped everyone through some pretty bad days - especially for those elderly people whose neighbours became their daily lifeline.

We are seeing neighbourhoods organising flood street parties and parish councils which provided bottled water thanking their volunteers. At all costs, we must hang on to this benefit that has come of the floody gloom. It is fact that without this sense of community and neighbourliness, Gloucestershire would not have survived its great flood of 2007 as well as it has done so far.

Ian Mean, Editor
The Citizen
October 2007

one

Deluge

A cyclist struggles through floodwaters in Sandford Park, Cheltenham. 790413-36

Friday, July 20

Warm air from a heatwave in continental Europe combined with cold air over the UK and formed a weather system off the south west coast of Britain. The system swept inland, first hitting south east England before swinging around towards Gloucestershire. It was the beginning of a natural disaster the likes of which the county had never seen before.

Rivers were already swollen after 27.6mm of rain on July 19 and the relentless rainfall showed no signs of abating.

Throughout the day 100.2mm of rain fell on Gloucestershire – three times the monthly average in just 17 hours. At 6.51pm the Environment Agency put the River Severn between Tewkesbury and Gloucester onto flood watch. Upstream between Worcester and Tewkesbury a flood warning was issued on the Severn and by 10.31pm the agency increased the warning to "severe."

Chaos reigned on county roads as the heaviest rain for 30 years wreaked havoc across Gloucestershire. The first reports of flooding came in at 7am and police were receiving 140 calls an hour. One county resident described the rain as being of "biblical proportions." At 3:29pm police set up a Silver Command at the Waterwells headquarters in Quedgeley with representatives from Gloucestershire Fire and Rescue Service, local authorities, the military and the Great Western Ambulance Service.

As the torrential rain refused to stop, the county's transport infrastructure was brought to a standstill. Evacuation on a huge scale was looking increasingly likely and stranded drivers began abandoning their vehicles as roads quickly became impassable.

At 6pm the police launched into their highest state of emergency management: Gold Command. The Gold team led by Gloucestershire Constabulary included Severn Trent Water, the Environment Agency, Central Networks, local authorities, the military and health agencies.

Across Gloucestershire a team of photographers from *The Citizen*, *Gloucestershire Echo* and *The Forester*, braved the treacherous conditions to capture the mayhem on camera.

College Road, Cheltenham, submerged by the rising waters. 750717-8

A car tries to drive through water at Elton Corner on the A48. 75328-10

Ashchurch, Tewkesbury. Within hours, the town would be surrounded by water. 730468-48

Opposite

Above left: Shoppers run for cover in Church Road, Bishop's Cleeve. 730468-4

Above right: Time to take a tea break for this resident in Hayward Road, Cheltenham. 790413-41

Bottom left: Felicity Hill and Remi Lanquetin make sandbags in College Road, Cheltenham. 750717-15

Bottom right: Smiling through the rain this man walks along flooded Prestbury High Street.

The Quay in Gloucester becomes a critical area as water levels continue to rise. 780653-18

Opposite

Above: Like hundreds of other motorists, this man is forced to abandon his vehicle after it became stranded at The Quay. 780653-5

Below: Drenched but defiant this woman struggles through the waters at The Quay, Gloucester. 780653-23

Above left: It's sandbags at dawn for Maria Rice at her home in Greyhound Gardens, Longlevens. 740716-8

Above right: Greyhound Gardens residents watch on, helpless, as the waters rise. www.swns.com

Left: Waiting for the worst to happen as water flows through Greyhound Gardens. www.swns.com

Opposite

Above: Joshua Myrans, 14, watches the drama unfold in Longlevens. 740716-13

Below: Water continues to rise throughout the day at Cypress Gardens, Longlevens. 740716-9

Above left: The depth of water is clearly visible in Cypress Gardens. 740716-5

Above right: Hayley Scott, Katie Williams and Laura Bartlett help out at a flooded home in Greyhound Gardens. 740716-19

Left: Terence Simmons deals with water dripping through the ceiling of his flat at The Dukeries, Gloucester. 780660-1

Opposite

Above: Beryl O'Reilly drives into trouble at The Quay. 780653-26

Below: Time to bail out for Beryl. 780653-29

Above: Children enjoy an impromptu paddle in Chipping Camden. 790413-53

Right: Watching the drama unfold from an upstairs window in High Street, Chipping Camden. 790413-62

Opposite

Above left: Members of the fire service help eachother draining their boots in Chipping Camden. 790413-13

Above right: Braving the waters in Chipping Camden. 790413-31

Below left: Time to abandon home as the rain falls incessantly on Chipping Camden. 790413-30

Below right: A fireman checks on shopkeepers in the flooded Cotswold town. 790413-8

Above and opposite: These dramatic pictures show just one of the many acts of courage during that fateful day on July 20. Motorist Graham Hancy, 42, had to be rescued from his car after it became stuck in six feet of water in Tredworth, Gloucester. Pictures by Bruce Seabrook, www.gpaimages.com

Above: Newlyweds Sarah and Andy Holtom were marooned along with 150 guests at Badgeworth Church as they tied the knot. www.swns.com

Above right: Remi Lanquetin bails out water after flooding in College Road, Cheltenham. 750717-20

Right: Prestbury High Street is hit by the flood. 730468-18

Opposite

Above: Leisure@Cheltenham, Tommy Taylors Lane, underwater.

Below: Motorcyclist Mark-Steen Adamson keeps steady along flooded Bath Road, Cheltenham. 750717-4

Above: Chaos on county roads continued through the day with scores of motorists forced to abandon their vehicles. Some even slept in their cars, unable to get home. On the A40 people pitched in to help others stranded by the water. www.swns.com

Left: Chaos on the A40.

Opposite page

Above: Gloucestershire Fire and Rescue Service arrive at Cypress Gardens, Longlevens. www.swns.com

Below: A *Gloucestershire Echo* reader captured the chaos at leisure@cheltenham.

Above: Slad Road in Stroud rapidly filled up with water during the day, Friday, July 20. 770641-12

Left: The depth of the water at Slad Road was incredible at the height of the flood. 770641-13

Opposite

Above: Stroud residents gather to watch the floods at The Painswick Inn. 770641-1

Below: The Swift Shop is deluged in Slad Road. 770641-9

Above: A car tries to plough through the floods on Bristol Road. 780662-11

Right: Smiling through the floods on Bristol Road, Gloucester. 780662-5

Opposite

Above: Locking Hill Surgery car park, Stroud. 770641-5

Below: The surgery car park completely submerged. 770641-2

Left: Water flows past the Morelands Trading Estate, Gloucester. 780662-13

Below: Cycling through the floods on Bristol Road after a day of torrential rain. 780662-3

two

Submerged

Saturday July 21

During the course of Saturday some sense of normality started to resume. The torrential rain had lifted and roads became passable again as water started to drain away. The majority of people had left rest centres and abandoned vehicles were collected. The main activity for the emergency services was providing support to those rescued. It appeared the emergency had passed and the county was now entering a recovery phase. This sense of normality however was short lived as the impact of the next unfolding event was realised by Gold Command.

At 02:45am on Sunday morning, the Mythe water treatment works in Tewkesbury was overwhelmed by floodwater resulting from the confluence of the Rivers Avon and Severn.

The Mythe was shut down to prevent any further damage and evacuated. The treatment centre provides drinking water to 150,000 properties in the county which meant 350,000 people across the majority of the county were soon going to lose their water supply, and it was clear it would amount to days before the supply could be re-commissioned.

Sunday July 22

Severn Trent Water had set up an emergency committee at its HQ in Coventry also sending a representative to join Gold. The Mythe was inaccessible and it was not clear when entry would be possible to even start making an assessment of the damage and timescales to resupply water.

As well as the problems at the Mythe, other situations were developing as a result of the rising water levels. The rapid rise of the River Severn around the Quay area in Gloucester necessitated the evacuation of homes in the area. A number of electricity substations in the Tewkesbury area needed to be shut down due to the floodwaters and the critical danger posed.

As the day progressed the attention of the emergency services turned to the Walham electricity switching station and Castlemeads substation in Gloucester. Both of these installations were being overwhelmed by floodwater, which had the potential to cause vast damage.

Castlemeads supplies electricity to 40,000 homes in south Gloucestershire. Walham supplies electricity to the majority of the county, large parts of Wales and parts of Bristol. The loss of this installation would be catastrophic to the county and the impact to communities without water supplies or electricity for a protracted period were unthinkable. Gloucestershire Fire and Rescue Service were using high volume pumps to displace the water, and the Environment Agency was arranging for the delivery of temporary flood defences. It was at this stage a formal request for military assistance was made. Severn Trent Water was making plans in relation to water distribution. Bottled water, and bowsers were being sourced.

Water had been supplied by tanker to local hospitals and 165 bowsers had been placed on the streets. People began bulk buying water – ironically because of fears over water supplies being contaminated by the floods. For thousands of residents the weekend was spent assessing the damage from the deluge on Friday. At Walham and Castlemeads a fierce battle was waged through the night to save the stations.

Monday July 23

While the Gold Command worked around the clock battling to save Walham across the county hundreds of people had to be rescued from the floods as the full extent of the crisis unfolded. The RNLI Rapid Response Unit worked tirelessly reaching scores of people stranded by the floods. Prime Minister Gordon Brown flew into the county to see for himself the devastation. He returned two days later to thank the emergency services for their valiant efforts.

Above and right: How *The Citizen* and *Gloucestershire Echo* covered the weekend's dramatic events.

Above: Rob Keene of Over Farm Market took to the skies in a microlight to capture this picture of the flooding at Over.

Left: The flooded waterworks at Mythe, Tewkesbury. Its closure left tens of thousands of homes in the county without fresh water.

Opposite

Some inmates had to be evacuated from Gloucester as water from the River Severn lapped around the jail. Photograph by South West News Service – www.swns.com

Above: One of the iconic pictures of
the floods showing Tewkesbury Abbey
surrounded by floodwaters. Photograph by
Barry Batchelor, Press Association

Right: Prime Minister Gordon Brown,
accompanied by Gloucester MP Parmjit
Dhanda, arrives in the county for the first
of two visits during the crisis. 750728-13

Opposite

Above: A caravan park in Tewkesbury
submerged under water. Photograph by
Barry Batchelor, Press Association.

Below: Tewkesbury was marooned by
the devastating floods. Photograph:
www.swns.com

Left: Residents in Longford brave the waters. 780672-27

Below: Stuart Rodway paddles through the Longford floods. 780672-22

Opposite

The RNLI Rapid Response Unit in action in Longford. 780672-20

Above: Firefighter Rowland Jones with eight-month-old Petie Rafferty who he rescued from the flooding at The Willows caravan site. 760290-19

Right: Little Micala Rafferty is helped off with her lifejacket after being rescued from The Willows.

Opposite

Above: Vicky Hawke and her children, Jack, three and Amber, six are rescued from their Sandhurst home along with Christina Serban and Pat Whitfield. 760290-8

Below: Rescue services speed into action along Sandhurst Lane. 780672-35

Above left: A woman walks carefully along Tewkesbury Road, Longford, one of the worst hit areas. 760289-3

Above right: Residents of The Willows in Sandhurst Lane putting on a brave face after being rescued. 760289-6

Left: The view from Westgate Bridge across to Oxleaze Meadow, Gloucester. 770651-4

Opposite

Above: This photograph of residents being evacuated from The Willows became the face of the Gloucestershire Flood Relief Fund which was set up to provide emergency money to victims of the disaster. 760289-8

Below: Sandhurst Lane where Woody the dog is rescued by Steve Cole who travelled from Churchdown to save the stranded pet.

Above: Westend Parade, Gloucester, under water.

Right: Scott Wain at his home in Westend Parade.
770649-10

Opposite

Above: Showman William Stevens, 76, at his home
in Pool Meadow, Gloucester. 770649-9

Below: Richard Perry surveys the damage at
his flooded home in Alney Terrace, Gloucester.
770649-2

Above: Nathan Wood helps with the clear-up at his home in Millham Road, Bishop's Cleeve. 740720-6

Left: The Salvation Army Citadel on Bath Road, Cheltenham where Andy Wilson helps with the aftermath of the floods. 720556-1

Opposite

Above: Rescuers pull Winchcombe resident Jo Ward to safety after she became trapped upstairs at her Castle Street home after the River Isbourne burst its banks.

Below: Gloucestershire Echo reader Abi Pates took this picture of the floods at Winchester Way, Cheltenham.

Above: Mark Gibbo, landlord of the Volunteer Inn, Chipping Camden, starts the clean-up operation after his cellar flooded. 790416-37

Left: Damage to the road in Mill Street, Prestbury. In total county roads suffered £25 million worth of damage. 740720-19

Opposite

Above: A Sea Rescue helicopter landing at Sandford Lido. Photograph by Clinton Mogridge.

Below: Severn Trent Water worker Dave Langley at Hewletts reservoir in Cheltenham. 750729-7

Above left: Tim and Francesca Hillier on the Dymock to Ledbury Road which collapsed due to the flooding. 780666-8

Above right: Frank Bayliss gets help from his daughter Corinna Tonks after the floods damaged furniture at his home on East Street, Moreton-in-Marsh. 790416-48

Left: Cotswold MP Geoffrey Clifton-Brown with councillor Sheila Jeffery survey the damage outside Philomena Adams' home. 790419-16

Opposite

Above: Muriel Swift at St David's School playing fields in Moreton-in-Marsh, trying to catch pet fish which had been swept out of their ponds. 790416-41

Below: Heather Jones cleaning up at the Dean Forest Hospice charity shop in Broad Street, Newent. 780665-6

Gloucester City Football Club's Meadow Park ground was devastated by the floods as these pictures by Neil Phelps illustrate.

Above left: Citizen reader Mark Playne took this photograph in Slad Road.

Above right: Cirencester Town's indoor football training facility was swamped by the floods. 720557-9

Right: Groundsman Brian Close kicks a ball around with Cirencester Town fan Kyle Chambers. 720557-3

Opposite

Above: Practice manager Jenny Vallely clears up at the Locking Hill Surgery in Stroud. 770642-16

Below: Mary Jones and Sue Roberts clear away mud from the Swift Shop in Slad Road, Stroud. 770642-2

Above left: The waters damaged the road in Stockwell Lane, Woodmancote. 740720-7

Above right: A resident in Westfield Terrace, Gloucester, climbs into his house using a ladder. 760291-2

Left: Over Farm Market on the A40 which was temporarily closed due to the flooding. 75332-2

Opposite

Above: Plock Court, Gloucester, completely submerged. 770664-8

Below: Baker Matt Flagg clearing up at The Sunshine Craft bakery, Stroud. 770642-11

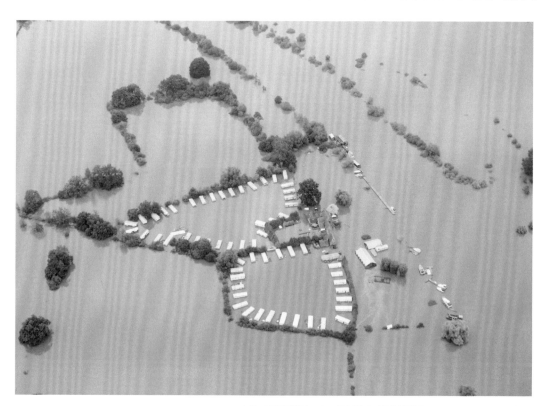

Above: Press Association's Kirsty Wrigglesworth took this dramatic shot of a caravan park near Tewkesbury.

Right: Taking a dip in Plock Court, Gloucester. 770664-2

Opposite

Above: Residents in Tewkesbury were completely isolated after the town was cut off on all sides. 740724-30

Below: Oldfield Road, Tewkesbury where the floodwaters stretched to the rear of the town's hospital. 740724-72

Right: Dean Mike Cogger looks at the flooded theatre at the Oxstalls campus of the University of Gloucestershire. 760293-2

Below: Residents at King John's Cottages on Mythe Road, Tewkesbury, battled to keep the floods at bay. Photograph by Stuart Strathearn.

Opposite

Craig Guthrie took these pictures at the height of the floods in Tewkesbury.

Overleaf

The Citizen and *Gloucestershire Echo* kept readers informed throughout the crisis. Hundreds of thousands of people also visited our website, www.thisisgloucestershire.co.uk, for minute by minute updates during the disaster.

Need A New Bathroom?
01452 330852
Severn Vale Bathrooms

GLOUCESTERSHIRE ECHO

EATING OUT token 1 offer

FREE Eating Out Guide worth £1.95 Token collect, p15

this is gloucestershire.co.uk   37p   Monday, July 23rd, 2007   FINAL

Water, water everywhere

. . . but not a drop to drink

- ■ **Taps run dry and power fails**
- ■ **Army guards electricity stations**
- ■ **PM Gordon Brown flies in**
- ■ **No water until Wednesday**
- ■ **Panic buying breaks out**
- ■ **Big clean-up under way**

Full story and pictures, Pages 1–9

NOW ENROLLING NEW PATIENTS

Independent prices less than NHS

Very high quality private dentistry

• Cosmetics and Surgical Treatment • Wrinkle Management and Sedation • Implants • Whitening

Smile Line Dental Centre 8, Libertus Road, Cheltenham. Call: 01242 523422

Need A New
Bathroom?
**01452
330852**
Severn Vale
Bathrooms

CITY FINAL

The Citizen

AT THE HEART OF GLOUCESTER

37p MONDAY, JULY 23, 2007

this is gloucestershire.co.uk

FREE
EATING OUT
1

Picture: Robert Davis 760289-8

■ **RESCUE:** Residents of Sandhurst are rescued by the fire service.

ON THE BRINK

■ Water supply set to run dry

■ Battle to save power substation

■ Rising river threatens city

■ Hundreds still left homeless

MORE floods have wreaked havoc in Gloucestershire, ruining homes and cutting off vital water and power supplies.

By Citizen reporters

citizen.news@glosmedia.co.uk

Thousands of people were expected to be without access to fresh water today as the swollen River Severn spilled out over the county leaving chaos in its wake.

Hundreds of water tanks were due to be drafted in with the water supply expected to be off in some areas until Wednesday.

LATEST ON THE FLOODING DEVASTATION: PAGES 2,3,4,5,6,7,8&9

NOW ENROLLING NEW PATIENTS

Independent prices less than NHS
Very high quality private dentistry
• Cosmetics and Surgical Treatment • Wrinkle Management and Sedation • Implants • Whitening

Smile Line Dental Centre 8, Libertus Road, Cheltenham. Call: 01242 523422

Right: Shoppers like Bob James of Highnam, stocked up on water and juice. 770647-5

Below: Yashar Nasser, a chef at Horton House nursing home in Gloucester collects water from a bowser. Photograph by Barry Batchelor, Press Association.

Opposite

Above: Severn Trent Water had distributed 239 bowsers by the end of Monday, July 23 after water supplies ran out. Alex Vittle fills up at The Cross, Gloucester. 760291-12

Below: A bowser at Rivermead Close, Sandhurst. 760290-1

Above: Gloucester residents flock to Tesco at Quedgeley where 150,000 free bottles of water are distributed. 780670-14

Left: Stocked up. 780670-12

Opposite

Above: Queues quickly built for the free water at Tesco in Quedgeley. 780670-5

Below left: Police in attendance as the water is given out. 780670-9

Below right: Officers co-ordinate the handout. 780670-1

Above: Mary Humphries and Siobahn Williams make soup at a support centre set up for flood victims at the Holy Trinity Church, Gloucester. Photograph by www.swns.com

Left: A dog paddles near Westgate Garage, Gloucester. 770651-13

three

Battle
Stations

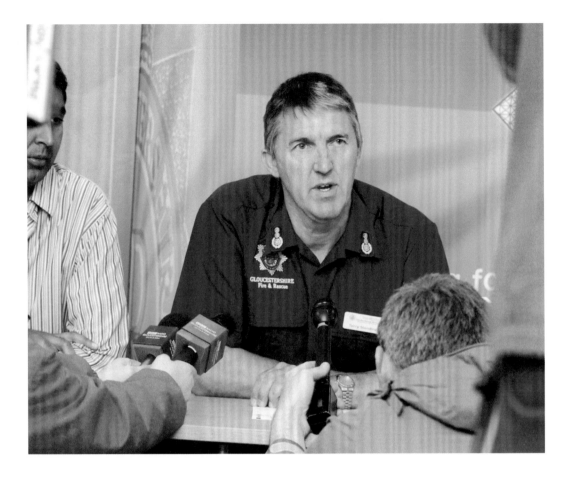

There were three key battle grounds during the first three days of the crisis: defending the Walham and Castlemeads electricity stations in Gloucester and the shutting down of the Mythe water treatment plant in Tewkesbury.

Here, Chief Fire Officer Terry Standing tells the epic tale of the "Battle for Walham. Our Trafalgar".

We had rescued some 600 people from boats alone during the Friday and Saturday (July 20-21) with all efforts being focused on saving lives of those in greatest danger. However, the storm was far from over.

On the Sunday afternoon we were committing a significant number of fire engines and pumps to the Walham National Grid Station. On the ground I had Kev Pottinger the Fire Incident Commander who had been battling rising floodwaters to save the site for some hours. This electrical station served some 600,000 people in Gloucestershire and also parts of Wales - to lose this battle would be catastrophic for people of Gloucestershire and would lead to deaths.

It was early afternoon and I was aware that the floodwater was rising fast, and our efforts were only just holding. Things were not looking good. I attended the Gold Command meeting and explained that the only way we were going to save this site was to get flood defences onsite, but I needed them quick. Tim Brain, the Chief Constable, recognised the importance of my demands and fully supported me.

Together, we took the critical decision to move Environment Agency flood defence equipment from Shropshire and Kidderminster to Walham immediately, and to support the Fire and Rescue Service with military personnel. If electricity was lost to the county, mass evacuation suddenly became a reality as all critical infrastructure reliant on electricity would fail including the remaining water pumping stations.

Right: A firefighter takes a well-earned rest at Castlemeads. 750731-4

Opposite

Gloucestershire Fire and Rescue Service Chief Fire Officer, Terry Standing, at an emergency press conference on Saturday, July 21.

Outside the Gold meeting a small group of us met with Tim and discussed the importance of the job in hand. Failure was not an option.

As I walked back to the Tri-Service Centre, I realised that this was probably going to be our biggest challenge. On meeting my Deputy, Chris Griffin, I emphasised the critical nature of the situation and immediately ordered all necessary resources to Walham. We desperately needed time for the flood defences to arrive by road, but time we didn't have.

By early evening, my firefighters and staff from other agencies were becoming tired. But all was not lost as the flood defence equipment finally arrived along with a Chinook helicopter full of Army personnel including 25 soldiers from the Ghurkha Regiment with 50 shovels supplied from Emergency Management Services to fill the increasing number of sandbags we needed. To make things worse, seven horses were stranded on the site and becoming increasingly distressed until they were captured and led to safety by RNLI crews.

Now we had a chance. We had the equipment and the personnel to save this site. Without hesitation I asked Chris Griffin, my deputy to go immediately to Walham and take charge. I knew we needed strong leadership to win this battle and Chris would get the very best out of my firefighters.

It was getting dark, water was still rapidly rising and racing across the site, where any work above head height could have been lethal as voltages of 400KV passed through a mass of wires, cables and transformers. A kilometre of flood defence barrier needed to be erected around the site and high tide was expected at around 5am.

It was vital to have in place the flood defence by that time. I had Fire Service 'High Volume' pumps standing by at the site and ready to move in. I telephoned Chris later that night for an up-date and he informed me that we were making progress but it was dangerous. With rising floodwater and now very dark, his people were disappearing into the darkness, safety of the personnel was becoming a real concern.

He had more than 100 people working within the site, flood water levels being constantly monitored by the RNLI. An evacuation signal had been agreed, as there was the capacity to rapidly rescue only 30 personnel, should the worst happen. My response to him was short and direct: "Chris we are not going to lose anyone tonight (meaning fatalities) but don't let me down, get the job done!" Chris fully understood the importance of the message.

At approximately 02.45hrs. a message came back to the Tri-Service Centre stating that the defence was in place and pumps were working at full power. High tide came and went and by 5am as dawn started to break crews were able to realise what they had achieved.

They had, in fact, done something never achieved before, they had erected a kilometre of flood defence in horrendous conditions in just four hours, the closest this had every been done before, in good condition, was eight hours. They had kept the lights on for Gloucestershire and I was extremely proud of what we had achieved.

Opposite

The Mythe water treatment works, flooded after convergence of the Severn and the Avon rivers. Inundated, the loss of the plant left 350,000 people without fresh water for up to 14 days. Picture: Ministry of Defence/Press Association.

Overleaf

Walham electricy switching station which supplies electricity to half a million homes in Gloucestershire. The night of Sunday July 22 saw the epicentre of the battle as emergency services and the military fought to protect the plant. Photograph by www.swns.com

Above: Crew from HMS *Campeltown* and HMS *Ocean* assisted in the operation to pump out water from Castlemeads. 780672-15

Right: A soldier carries a sandbag at Castlemeads. 780672-4

Opposite

Castlemeads electricity substation in Gloucester is swamped by the floods. www.swns.com

Above: Gloucestershire Highways staff help during the crisis at Castlemeads. 780672-17

Left: Pumping out Castlemeads which supplies electricity to 40,000 homes. 780672-5

Opposite

Above: Floodwater blasts out from the stricken substation. 780672-1

Below: The Lord Lt of Gloucestershire, Henry Elwes, accompanied by Chief Fire Officer, Terry Standing, talk to firefighters at Castlemeads. 760294-1

Left: Prime Minister Gordon Brown visiting Walham on Wednesday, July 25. 780683-16

Below: Inside the battleground at Walham. 760292-1

Opposite

Thousands of sandbags and a kilometre of flood defences were erected around Walham. If the battle had been lost it would have led to mass evacuation of large parts of Gloucestershire to Birmingham and Bristol. Photograph by www.swns.com

Above: Trevor Perryman and Roy Billings shore up defences at Walham. 760292-8

Left: Firefighter Frederick Le Ouedic tends to the defence barrier at Walham. 760292-6

Opposite

Time to celebrate for some of the valiant team who saved Walham. 760292-5

Above: A barrier was built under incredibly challenging, dangerous conditions. Photograph by www.swns.com

Left: Tally Giampa of Gloucestershire Fire and Rescue Service inside Walham. Tally has his finger on the level reached by the floods. Two more inches and the station would have been shut down. 780736-1

Opposite

Above: The flooded waterworks at Mythe. Photograph by www.swns.com

Below: Pumping out at Mythe. 790420-4

Above: Inside the devastated Mythe water treatment plant. 730478-4

Left: Mike Bishop of Severn Trent Water inspecting the ongoing repair work at Mythe. Photograph by www.swns.com

Opposite

Above: Inside the stricken treatment plant at Mythe. Photograph by www.swns.com

Below: Base camp for the repair effort at Mythe. 790420-3

Above: One week after the floods the water retreats from Mythe. Photograph by www.swns.com

Left: After the battle to save power the crisis turned to water shortages across Gloucestershire. Mike Bowkett, site manager at Mythe, gives advice about saving water. 234837-9

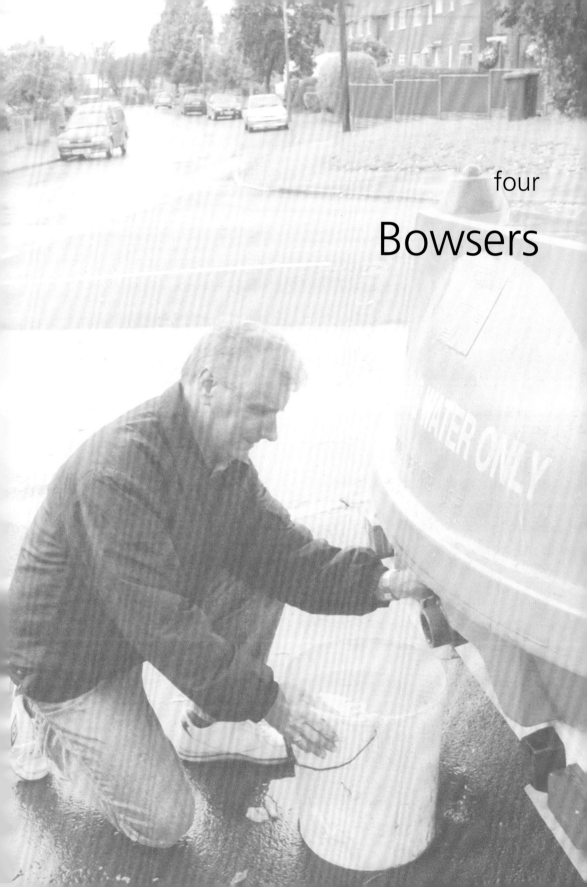

four

Bowsers

After the devastating rains and the battles to protect power, the disaster had a new focus – water shortages.

Supplies to 150,000 homes had been wiped out by the closure of Mythe and it would be at least 14 days before they returned. The loss of water had huge implications for homes and businesses across the county – many of which were still deluged by floodwaters. More than 5,000 homes had been flooded and more than 50 schools had also suffered damage.

By the end of Monday, July 23, 239 bowsers had been distributed and a further 900 were already planned.

Cheltenham Racecourse became the epicentre of the effort to distribute bowsers and bottled water over the coming days. The Royal Logistics Corps were working with Severn Trent to manage the mass distribution.

By the end of Tuesday, July 24, a total of 700 bowsers were on the streets and millions of litres of bottled water were being distributed from key sites across the county – but it wasn't enough.

Thousands of people logged onto www.thisisgloucestershire.co.uk where the locations of bowsers were constantly updated but many emailed in saying the bowsers were always empty.

On Thursday, July 26 the Strensham valve was opened bringing water to the majority of homes in Tewkesbury. However the water was not safe to drink and there was a long way to go before the crisis was over.

By Saturday July 28 there were 1,450 bowsers on the streets, 10.2 million litres of bottled water was in stock with a further 20 million litres on order.

The defence bastion around Mythe was 98 per cent complete and a predicted heavy rainfall on the Saturday did not materialise with only 5-10mm falling.

By Thursday, August 2, 100 per cent of county residents had fresh water supplies and at 5pm the next day a press conference was held to say water was now fit to drink if boiled.

On Monday, August 6, Gloucestershire Constabulary formally decided that the emergency phase of the disaster – Operation Outlook – was now over and on Tuesday, August 7 Severn Trent Water announced that tap water was now safe to drink.

Left: Anita Tarawneh and daughter Yasmine use a bowser in Hewlett Road, Cheltenham. 750738

Opposite

Empty bowsers were a familiar feature during the early days of the operation to keep Gloucestershire supplied with water. Photograph by www.swns.com

Above: Trucks packed with water arrive at Cheltenham Racecourse. 790423-20

Left: Millions of litres of bottled water stored at the racecourse during the water shortage. 790423-22

Opposite

Above left and right: How *The Gloucestershire Echo* and *The Citizen* covered the water crisis.

Below: Stretching as far as the eye can see – bottled water ready for distribution. 790423-25

95

Left: A family fill up at Rowanfield, Cheltenham. 740729-2

Below: Bowsers stored and filled at Staverton. 730579-7

Opposite

HRH Prince Charles and Chief Fire Officer Terry Standing visiting the relief effort at Cheltenham Racecourse. 740736-21

Left: A pensioner fills up from a bowser in Hester's Way, Cheltenham. Photograph by www.swns.com

Below: Residents using the bowser at Grange Road, Tuffley, Gloucester. 770667-6

Opposite

Above: Soldiers planning the distribution operation at Cheltenham Racecourse. 790423-21

Below: Morgan and Ellis Boon frustrated at the empty bowser in Abbeydale. 780681-3

Above: Residents find a full bowser in Milton Avenue, Gloucester. 770667-1

Left: Yacob Tily delivers water to Usuf Ginwalla, 80 in the Barton Street area of Gloucester. 780680-4

Opposite

Above: Barman Dave Rhodes enjoys a pint of water outside the Lamb Inn, Eastcombe, which had to shut during the crisis. 770664-3

Below: Army trucks roll into Cheltenham Racecourse. Photograph by Anthony Devlin, Press Association.

Right: Freya Chambers, three, collecting water from Bisley Wells. 770666-8

Below left: Beverley Nash at Bisley Wells. 770666-6

Below right: Flood Recovery Minister John Healey speaks to council worker Dave Hull at Spring Gardens car park, Tewkesbury. 790422-16

Opposite

Above: Residents in Bishop's Cleeve collect water at Tesco. 710229-1

Below: PC Bryan Griffiths and Neighbourhood Warden Peter Gleed hand out water at Waitrose in Stroud. 770665-3

Above: Victims of the water shortage at Tesco in Gloucester. Photograph by Anthony Devlin, Press Association.

Left: Andrew Field in Shelley Road, Cheltenham. 740729-5

Opposite

Above: PC Michelle Bond, who helped to save a girl from drowning during the floods, hands out water at Sainsbury's, Tewkesbury Road, Cheltenham. 740729-6

Below: Sisters Sasha, Georgia and Collette pick up water at Tesco in Gloucester. Photograph by www.swns.com

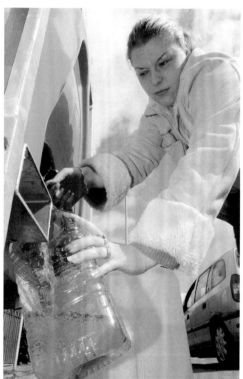

Above: Councillor Andy Gravells joins residents in Abbeydale to express concern over empty bowsers – but the misery was soon to end. 780681-2

Left: Tina Trigg fills up at a bowser in Quedgeley. 780673-2

Opposite

Above: Sisters Sophia and Elysia Byrne from Longlevens celebrate the return of safe drinking water. 750773-10

Below: Sam White, water quality inspector for Severn Trent Water examining a sample. 720586-1

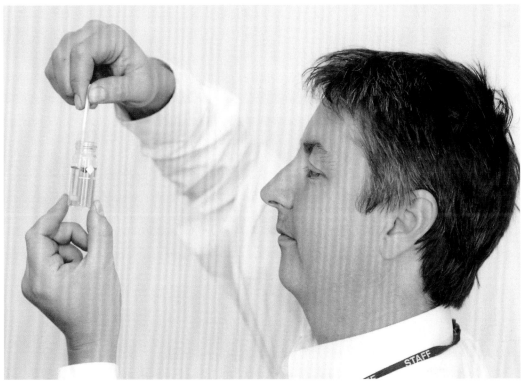

Lydia Taylor, 18 months, with water collected from the former B&Q site in Gloucester.

Chief Constable Dr Tim Brain at one of the daily press conferences held at Waterwells, Quedgeley. 770643-10

Gloucestershire Constabulary's Chief Constable, Dr Tim Brain, gives his account of the biggest peacetime disaster ever to unfold in the county:

None of us will ever forget the events of July 20 and the days and weeks that followed. We and colleagues in partner agencies have been planning and training for a host of crisis situations for many years. However, the largest peacetime emergency ever recorded in this country presented many challenges.

The Constabulary is responsible for co-ordinating the overall response to major incidents in Gloucestershire. The immense amount of rain which fell that Friday had an immediate impact on properties and the road network. It quickly became apparent that we would need to invoke our standard Bronze, Silver, and Gold structure of dealing with such emergencies.

Our Silver Command started up at 3.30 that first afternoon, initially involving just ourselves and the fire and ambulance services.

Without doubt, we benefited from having one of the only Tri-Service centres in the country and we were able to quickly co-ordinate a joint response to the severe flooding and the stranding of motorists. The situation steadily worsened and by 6pm we were setting up Gold Command at our headquarters in Waterwells, Quedgeley.

The focus of the emergency effort in the early stages was on the preservation of life and property, rescuing and evacuating those stranded in their homes or vehicles and dealing with immense traffic problems. As the early hours of Sunday July 22 dawned, other problems presented themselves. The Mythe water treatment plant was overcome by water, and the following day power was lost to tens of thousands of homes when electricity substations were powered down due to the threat of flooding.

An even worse catastrophe was threatened when we found water was encroaching around substations at Walham and Castlemeads. With Castlemeads supplying electricity to around 40,000 homes and Walham supplying homes countywide, as well as parts of Wales and Bristol, the loss of these installations would be devastating. Realising the potential scale of the situation we invoked arrangements giving us military aid and began dialogue with the Cabinet Office Briefing Room (COBR).

In the following days the two issues at the forefront of our minds were getting water to the 350,000 people without a mains supply, and safeguarding the substations.

On Monday the Army arrived en masse and Brigadier Jolyon Jackson joined us in Gold to prioritise what we could do to save Walham. We also worked with central Government to bring in large pumps and barriers. At the same time we were working with Severn Trent to plan bowser and water distribution on a massive and urgent scale.

At the height of the emergency Gold was meeting every four to five hours and in between that I was briefing COBR with updates.

All of the agencies had representatives at Waterwells, and we worked together tirelessly 24 hours a day to deal with a range of issues to try and restore a form of normality to county residents.

The turning point didn't come until Thursday when we knew Walham was saved, Castlemeads was back on line and engineers had begun working at Mythe. The distribution plan for bottled water, devised by the military and Severn Trent, was making an impact and the number of bowsers and the rate at which they were being refilled were significantly higher. Soon afterwards water began flowing back through taps and, while there were still problems to be solved, such as making the temporary flood defences at the key installations more permanent, the worst of the crisis was over. Of course we know that for many county householders and business owners it will be a long time until they are able to return to normality.

As we reflect back on what we dealt with we can be rightly proud of what we achieved and delivered. We are a small force but we have proved that we have the strategic capability, resources and skills to lead such an emergency effectively while continuing to meet the demands of day-to-day policing.

I am extremely proud of the officers and staff who worked long hours both on the ground and behind the scenes despite, in several cases, having suffered from the flooding themselves.

We will, of course, now be reviewing our response, but our communities can feel reassured that the force has the capability and flexibility to deal with the biggest of emergency scenarios. The investment the Police Authority has made in the Constabulary over recent years has provided us with the necessary infrastructure to command and co-ordinate such incidents.

I am grateful to all the other agencies that worked with us during this joint response, as well as the residents of this county who showed great fortitude and forbearance throughout.

Dr Brain briefs Prime Minister Gordon Brown as he visits Waterwells with Gloucester MP Parmjit Dhanda. 750728-6

five

Relief

After the floods had gone and fresh water supplies were back on, thousands of householders began to count the cost of the devastation. More than 5,000 homes were affected by the floods as well as scores of county businesses. Something had to be done.

The Mayor of Gloucester Harjit Gill and the Mayor of Tewkesbury, Phil Awford, along with *The Citizen*, *Gloucestershire Echo* and *The Forester*, launched the Gloucestershire Flood Relief Fund.

Within hours of the fund being launched businesses had pledged more than a quarter of a million pounds. Within a few days that had risen to over £600,000. Across the county people began organizing fund raising events and the money kept pouring in to help the victims of the floods.

The Citizen, *Gloucestershire Echo* and www.thisisgloucestershire.co.uk drove the campaign across the county and the money was still pouring in when this book went to press.

Parmjit Dhanda, MP for Gloucester, Cllr Phil Awford, Mayor of Tewkesbury, Cllr Harjit Gill, Mayor of Gloucester, Right Reverend Michael Perham, Bishop of Gloucester and Cllr Paul James, Leader of Gloucester City Council, at the launch of the Gloucestershire Flood Relief Fund.

Opposite

A poster produced by Gloucestershire Media to promote the flood fund.

GLOUCESTERSHIRE

FLOOD RELIEF FUND

YOU CAN MAKE YOUR DONATION AT ANY HSBC  BRANCH

The Citizen   GLOUCESTERSHIRE ECHO   The Forester

Above: Simon Taylor surveys the damage at his home in Alney Terrace, Gloucester. Photograph by www.swns.com

Left: Michelle Hicks collects money for the fund from Tewkesbury resident Derek Watson. 740787-4

Opposite

Station manager Phil Ryan is given a helping hand by Rhys Hughes, six, while collecting for the Gloucestershire Flood Relief Fund in Tewkesbury. 740787-5

Above left: Mike Reeves, 69, playing the organ in the Eastgate Mall, Gloucester, to raise money for flood victims. 780748-5

Above right: Holly Brown at Norwood News in Cheltenham with a collection bottle. 740751-1

Left: Angela Sim from British Energy. The firm donated £10,000 to the fund. 750775-9

Opposite

Above: Dancing at the start of the Gloucestershire's Severn Sound Dance 1000 event held in Gloucester Park raising thousands of pounds for the relief fund. 780723-6

Below: Lynda Howell, Rich Preece and Urszula Przybysz-Pereira of Barclays Bank, Eastgate Street, Gloucester, dressed up to raise money for the fund. 750761-4

Above: Rob Keene of Over Farm Market sits astride a submerged tractor. The floods devastated his potato crop. 74340-7

Right: Pauline Jeffries, warehouse manager at Brynteg Books, with her daughter Heidi Finch, assessing the damage. A total of £250,000 worth of stock was damaged in the floods. 740730-1

Opposite

Above: Klaus Pittaway surveys the damage at his Alney Terrace home. Photograph by www.swns.com

Below: Coyeta Brown takes in the flood damage at Alney Terrace. Photograph by www.swns.com

Left: Mukesh Patel at Krishna News in Churchdown, supporting the Gloucestershire Flood Relief Fund. 740753-2

Below: Butlers pub in Eastgate Street, Gloucester, joins in the fundraising drive. Manager Justin Hudson with a bucket ready to collect. 750760-1

Opposite

Above: HSBC employees Kasia Hejnar, Amy D'Ambrogio, Kate Simpson, Nicola Vizard and Gemma Green, outside the Gloucester branch, celebrating the fund reaching £500,000. 790479-2

Below: Malkit, Khem, nine months, and Randip Padda at M&R Stores in Longlevens, join the fundraising effort. Photograph by Antony Thompson. www.atp-photo.com

Left: Anne Regan and Stephen Petherick stand by the flood damaged pool at leisure@cheltenham, Tommy Taylor's Lane. 740728-6

Below: Flood victim Sandra Buckland cleaning up after her Severn Road, Cheltenham, home was flooded. 740727-3.

Opposite

Above: Longford evacuee, Brindley Davies, 101, relaxes at the Ramada Hotel in Matson. 780674-2

Below: Ron Horn and his wife Anne outside their flooded shop in Chipping Campden. 750733-3

Above: The Bishop of Gloucester, Michael Perham, visits St Stephens Church, Bristol Road, Gloucester, to offer support after the floods. 770660-6

Left: Monika Blaszczyk of HSBC promoting the Gloucestershire Flood Relief Fund, which the bank supported. 740759-2

Opposite

Above: Steve Rainer cleans up at the Sue Ryder Care shop in Sherbourne Street, Bourton-on-the-Water. 750732-2

Below: Gloucester All Blues rugby football club Treasurer Gary Teague with President George Lewis and Rob Hart, Secretary, after the floods. 780682-1

Above: Mia Ward splashes around the floodwaters in Longford. 780676-3

Opposite

Above and below: Tewkesbury, before and after the flood. Photograph by www.swns.com

If you would like to purchase any of the photographs in this book please contact Gloucestershire Media on 01242 271822 quoting the reference number of the photograph you would like to buy.

You can also have the photograph printed on mugs, mouse mats, T-shirts and coasters.